SCHOLASTIC

FunnyBone
BOOKS®

DIVISION
PRACTICE PUZZLES

40 Reproducible Solve-the-Riddle Activity Pages
That Help All Kids Master Division

by Bob Hugel

NEW YORK • TORONTO • LONDON • AUCKLAND • SYDNEY
MEXICO CITY • NEW DELHI • HONG KONG • BUENOS AIRES

Teaching *Resources*

Dedication

To Donovan, my superhero

Cover design by Maria Lilja
Cover illustration by Kelly Kennedy
Interior design by Holly Grundon
Interior illustrations by Jack Desrocher

ISBN 0-439-51376-6
Copyright © 2005 by Bob Hugel
All rights reserved.
Printed in the U.S.A.

2 3 4 5 6 7 8 9 10   40   12 11 10 09 08 07 06

Contents

Introduction

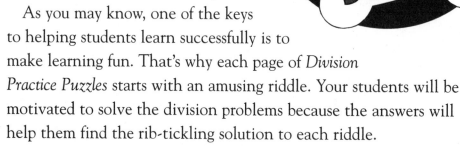

Welcome to *FunnyBone Books: Division Practice Puzzles*, a surefire way to get students excited about math. This book combines basic division problems with loads of hilarious riddles guaranteed to get students revved up for learning.

As you may know, one of the keys to helping students learn successfully is to make learning fun. That's why each page of *Division Practice Puzzles* starts with an amusing riddle. Your students will be motivated to solve the division problems because the answers will help them find the rib-tickling solution to each riddle.

Along the way, your students will be drilled on several division skills, including dividing whole numbers, working with remainders, and solving division word problems. We hope your students enjoy *Division Practice Puzzles* and benefit from the skills presented in this book.

By making learning about division enjoyable, we hope to reveal a wonderful secret to your students—math is lots of fun!

NAME _____ DATE _____

Riddle 1

Why is heat faster than cold?

What To Do

Solve the division problems below. Match each quotient to a letter in the Key. Then write the letter in the space above its problem number to find the answer to the riddle.

1 1 ÷ 1 = _____   **6** 2 ÷ 1 = _____

2 4 ÷ 1 = _____   **7** 8 ÷ 1 = _____

3 3 ÷ 1 = _____   **8** 6 ÷ 1 = _____

4 9 ÷ 1 = _____   **9** 5 ÷ 1 = _____

5 7 ÷ 1 = _____   **10** 10 ÷ 1 = _____

Key

5 C	15 V	0 . . . . W
12 . . . . M	1 C	9 . . . . T
4 L	14 I	11 . . . . B
8 . . . . A	7 . . . . O	6 . . . . D
10 . . . . . . H	3 C	2 . . . . A

Riddle Answer

You can ___ ___ ___ ___ ___ ___ ___ ___ ___ ___ .

9 **7** **4** **1** **10**   **6**   **3** **5** **2** **8**

NAME_____ DATE_____

Riddle 2

Why do bats always stay in groups?

What To Do

Solve the division problems below. Match each quotient to a letter in the Key. Then write the letter in the space above its problem number to find the answer to the riddle.

1   6 ÷ 2 = _____   **6**   18 ÷ 2 = _____

2   2 ÷ 2 = _____   **7**   8 ÷ 2 = _____

3   10 ÷ 2 = _____   **8**   12 ÷ 2 = _____

4   4 ÷ 2 = _____   **9**   16 ÷ 2 = _____

5   14 ÷ 2 = _____   **10**   20 ÷ 2 = _____

Key

0 .... P	1 .... T	7 .... O
6 .... E	2 .... H	20 .... U
4 .... R	15 .... S	8 .... G
5 .... E	9 .... N	10 .... G
12 .... A	14 .... K	3 .... T

Riddle Answer

They like to ha __ __ __ __ __ __ __ __ __ __ .
     6 **10**   **2** **5** **9** **8** **1** **4** **3** **7**

NAME_____ DATE_____

Riddle 3

Why did the golfer carry extra socks?

What To Do

Solve the division problems below. Match each quotient to a letter in the Key. Then write the letter in the space above its problem number to find the answer to the riddle.

① 3 ÷ 3 = _____   ⑥ 18 ÷ 3 = _____
② 6 ÷ 3 = _____   ⑦ 21 ÷ 3 = _____
③ 9 ÷ 3 = _____   ⑧ 24 ÷ 3 = _____
④ 12 ÷ 3 = _____   ⑨ 27 ÷ 3 = _____
⑤ 15 ÷ 3 = _____   ⑩ 30 ÷ 3 = _____

Key

4 I	7 . . . . H	12 . . . . R
20 . . . . W	1 . . . . E	3 . . . . N
6 . . . . O	15 . . . . M	11 C
0 . . . . P	2 L	9 . . . . N
8 . . . . A	5 . . . . E	10 . . . . O

Riddle Answer

In case she got ___ ___ ___ ___ ___ ___ ___ ___ ___ ___
⑧   ⑦ ⑥ ② ⑤   ④ ⑨   ⑩ ③ ①

NAME_____ DATE_____

Riddle 4

Why did the witch's hair stay in place?

What To Do

Solve the division problems below. Match each quotient to a letter in the Key. Then write the letter in the space above its problem number to find the answer to the riddle.

1   8 ÷ 4 = _____   **6**   32 ÷ 4 = _____

2   4 ÷ 4 = _____   **7**   40 ÷ 4 = _____

3   24 ÷ 4 = _____   **8**   16 ÷ 4 = _____

4   36 ÷ 4 = _____   **9**   28 ÷ 4 = _____

5   12 ÷ 4 = _____   **10**   20 ÷ 4 = _____

Key

16 . . . . F	25 . . . . U	2 . . . . Y
6 . . . . S	5 . . . . R	3 . . . . R
4 . . . . P	10 . . . . S	0 . . . . N
12 . . . . T	1 . . . . E	9 . . . . A
7 C	22 L	8 . . . . A

Riddle Answer

She put on ___ ___ ___ ___ ___ ___ ___ ___ ___ ___ .

3 **9** **6** **10** **2**   **7** **8** **5** **4** **1**

NAME _____ **DATE** _____

Riddle 5

Why is a fish easy to weigh?

What To Do

Solve the division problems below. Match each quotient to a letter in the Key. Then write the letter in the space above its problem number to find the answer to the riddle.

1 35 ÷ 5 = _____   **6** 5 ÷ 5 = _____

2 10 ÷ 5 = _____   **7** 45 ÷ 5 = _____

3 30 ÷ 5 = _____   **8** 15 ÷ 5 = _____

4 25 ÷ 5 = _____   **9** 40 ÷ 5 = _____

5 20 ÷ 5 = _____   **10** 50 ÷ 5 = _____

Key

12 . . . . R	3 . . . . S	15 . . . . B
20 . . . . M	19 . . . . W	8 . . . . E
5 . . . . S	9 . . . . A	14 . . . . P
10 C	2 . . . . W	4 . . . . S
1 . . . . N	7 . . . . O	6 L

Riddle Answer

It has it ___ ___ ___ ___ ___ ___ ___ ___ ___ ___ .
  4   **1** **2** **6** **8** **10** **7** **3** **9** **5**

NAME _____ DATE _____

Riddle 6

What did the bees put on when they were cold?

What To Do

Solve the division problems below. Match each quotient to a letter in the Key. Then write the letter in the space above its problem number to find the answer to the riddle.

1 12 ÷ 6 = _____

2 6 ÷ 6 = _____

3 60 ÷ 6 = _____

4 48 ÷ 6 = _____

5 18 ÷ 6 = _____

6 54 ÷ 6 = _____

7 36 ÷ 6 = _____

8 24 ÷ 6 = _____

9 30 ÷ 6 = _____

10 42 ÷ 6 = _____

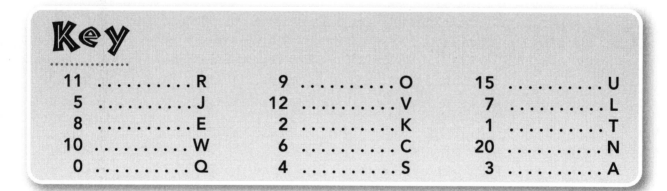

Key

11 .... R	9 .... O	15 .... U
5 .... J	12 V	7 L
8 .... E	2 .... K	1 .... T
10 .... W	6 C	20 .... N
0 .... Q	4 .... S	3 .... A

Riddle Answer

Their yel __ __ __   __ __ __ __ __ __ __
　　　　　　　⑩ ⑥ ③　⑨ ⑤ ⑦ ① ④ ② ⑧

NAME _____   DATE _____

Riddle 7

Why did the pig break into the house?

What To Do

Solve the division problems below. Match each quotient to a letter in the Key. Then write the letter in the space above its problem number to find the answer to the riddle.

1 35 ÷ 7 = _____

2 49 ÷ 7 = _____

3 28 ÷ 7 = _____

4 63 ÷ 7 = _____

5 56 ÷ 7 = _____

6 14 ÷ 7 = _____

7 70 ÷ 7 = _____

8 7 ÷ 7 = _____

9 21 ÷ 7 = _____

10 42 ÷ 7 = _____

Key

9 . . . . B	6 . . . . R	18 I
14 . . . . P	10 . . . . A	7 . . . . G
24 . . . . W	11 . . . . K	4 . . . . U
3 . . . . M	2 L	12 I
1 . . . . R	5 . . . . H	8 . . . . A

Riddle Answer

He was a __ __ __ - __ __ __ __ __ __ __.

1 **7** **9** **4** **3** **8** **2** **6** **5** **10**

NAME _____ DATE _____

Riddle 8

How do elephants talk to one another?

What To Do

Solve the division problems below. Match each quotient to a letter in the Key. Then write the letter in the space above its problem number to find the answer to the riddle.

1 72 ÷ 8 = _____   **6** 64 ÷ 8 = _____

2 56 ÷ 8 = _____   **7** 24 ÷ 8 = _____

3 32 ÷ 8 = _____   **8** 48 ÷ 8 = _____

4   8 ÷ 8 = _____   **9** 80 ÷ 8 = _____

5 16 ÷ 8 = _____   **10** 40 ÷ 8 = _____

Key

25 ....J	7 ....P	6 ....E
3 ....O	15 ....B	12 ....F
5 ....N	1 ....E	2 L
20 ....A	8 ....E	0 ....G
10 ....H	9 ....E	4 ....S

Riddle Answer

They us __ ' __ __ __ __ __ __ __ __ __ .
    1   **6** **5** **8** **2** **9** **7** **10** **4** **3**

NAME _____   DATE _____

Riddle 9

How did people greet the boy who was named after his father?

What To Do

Solve the division problems below. Match each quotient to a letter in the Key. Then write the letter in the space above its problem number to find the answer to the riddle.

1 36 ÷ 9 = _____   **6** 18 ÷ 9 = _____

2 9 ÷ 9 = _____   **7** 27 ÷ 9 = _____

3 45 ÷ 9 = _____   **8** 81 ÷ 9 = _____

4 90 ÷ 9 = _____   **9** 54 ÷ 9 = _____

5 63 ÷ 9 = _____   **10** 72 ÷ 9 = _____

Key

13 . . . . M	1 . . . . D	6 . . . . O
7 . . . . D	8 . . . . H	16 C
2 . . . . D	14 . . . . B	9 . . . . W
10 . . . . Y	5 . . . . A	15 . . . . N
18 . . . . K	4 . . . . Y	3 . . . . D

Riddle Answer

___ ___ ___ ___ ___ , ___ ___ ___ ___ ___ ___ !
10 **9** **8** **6** **1**   **2** **3** **5** **7** **4**

NAME _____ DATE _____

Riddle 10

Why did the Girl Scout get dizzy?

What To Do

Solve the division problems below. Match each quotient to a letter in the Key. Then write the letter in the space above its problem number to find the answer to the riddle.

1   50 ÷ 10 = _____   **6**   80 ÷ 10 = _____

2   70 ÷ 10 = _____   **7**   20 ÷ 10 = _____

3   100 ÷ 10 = _____   **8**   30 ÷ 10 = _____

4   90 ÷ 10 = _____   **9**   10 ÷ 10 = _____

5   40 ÷ 10 = _____   **10**   60 ÷ 10 = _____

Key

5 .... T	12 .... F	4 .... R
15 .... Y	2 .... N	8 .... S
10 .... U	0 C	22 .... R
3 .... G	19 .... Q	1 .... D
9 .... O	7 .... G	6 .... O

Riddle Answer

She spent all day doin ___   ___ ___ ___ ___ ___   ___ ___ ___ ___ ___.

      8   **2** **4** **10** **9**   **1** **3** **5** **7** **6**

NAME _____   DATE _____

Riddle 11

Why did the chicken cross the Internet?

What To Do

Solve the division problems below. Match each quotient to a letter in the Key. Then write the letter in the space above its problem number to find the answer to the riddle.

① 44 ÷ 2 = _____   **⑥** 72 ÷ 2 = _____

② 54 ÷ 2 = _____   **⑦** 76 ÷ 2 = _____

③ 62 ÷ 2 = _____   **⑧** 52 ÷ 2 = _____

④ 58 ÷ 2 = _____   **⑨** 64 ÷ 2 = _____

⑤ 66 ÷ 2 = _____   **⑩** 78 ÷ 2 = _____

Key

33 . . . . E	32 . . . . R	26 . . . . O
30 . . . . A	27 . . . . S	31 . . . . T
22 . . . . H	24 C	37 . . . . M
39 I	38 . . . . E	29 . . . . E
23 . . . . B	25 . . . . D	36 . . . . T

Riddle Answer

It wanted to get to th ___ ___ ___ ___ ___ ___ ___ ___ ___ ___.

 **④** **⑧** **⑥** **①** **⑤** **⑨** **②** **⑩** **③** **⑦**

Division Practice Puzzles **15**

NAME_____   DATE_____

Riddle 12

Why did the bee hum?

What To Do

Solve the division problems below. Match each quotient to a letter in the Key. Then write the letter in the space above its problem number to find the answer to the riddle.

1 $36 \div 3 =$ _____   **6** $33 \div 3 =$ _____

2 $45 \div 3 =$ _____   **7** $42 \div 3 =$ _____

3 $51 \div 3 =$ _____   **8** $39 \div 3 =$ _____

4 $54 \div 3 =$ _____   **9** $48 \div 3 =$ _____

5 $60 \div 3 =$ _____   **10** $57 \div 3 =$ _____

Key

23 . . . . M	16 . . . . S	17 . . . . S
18 . . . . R	11 . . . . D	20 . . . . W
14 . . . . N	24 . . . . K	15 . . . . O
7 C	19 . . . . S	5 V
13 . . . . G	32 . . . . A	12 . . . . O

Riddle Answer

It forgot the ___ ___ ___ ___ ___ ' ___ ___ ___ ___ ___ ___ .
9 **2** **7** **8** **10** **5** **1** **4** **6** **3**

NAME_____   DATE_____

Riddle 13

Why did the bird visit the library?

What To Do

Solve the division problems below. Match each quotient to a letter in the Key. Then write the letter in the space above its problem number to find the answer to the riddle.

1 50 ÷ 2 = _____   **6** 66 ÷ 6 = _____

2 72 ÷ 2 = _____   **7** 78 ÷ 6 = _____

3 63 ÷ 3 = _____   **8** 90 ÷ 6 = _____

4 84 ÷ 3 = _____   **9** 72 ÷ 6 = _____

5 81 ÷ 3 = _____   **10** 84 ÷ 6 = _____

Key

22 . . . . A	20 . . . . Q	75 . . . . N
12 . . . . O	80 V	15 . . . . O
11 . . . . W	21 . . . . B	13 L
45 . . . . J	28 . . . . S	27 . . . . R
25 . . . . M	36 . . . . K	14 . . . . O

Riddle Answer

It was ____ **ooking for** __ __ __ __ __ __ __ __ __ .

7   **3** **9** **10** **2** **6** **8** **5** **1** **4**

NAME _____   DATE _____

Riddle 14

Why was the girl worried when her nose grew to be 11 inches long?

What To Do

Solve the division problems below. Match each quotient to a letter in the Key. Then write the letter in the space above its problem number to find the answer to the riddle.

1 24 ÷ 2 = _____

2 60 ÷ 2 = _____

3 36 ÷ 2 = _____

4 40 ÷ 2 = _____

5 28 ÷ 2 = _____

6 44 ÷ 4 = _____

7 52 ÷ 4 = _____

8 60 ÷ 4 = _____

9 68 ÷ 4 = _____

10 76 ÷ 4 = _____

Key

11 .... N	19 .... O	15 .... T
16 .... R	24 .... E	20 I
14 .... F	30 .... N	8 .... Z
13 .... O	18 .... A	17 .... O
21 .... P	7 .... Q	12 .... T

Riddle Answer

She thought it might tur __ __ __ __ __ __ __ __ __ __ __ .

NAME _____   DATE _____

Riddle 15

Which flower did the bee like best?

What To Do

Solve the division problems below. Match each quotient to a letter in the Key. Then write the letter in the space above its problem number to find the answer to the riddle.

1 88 ÷ 4 = _____   **6** 48 ÷ 8 = _____

2 56 ÷ 4 = _____   **7** 96 ÷ 8 = _____

3 64 ÷ 4 = _____   **8** 32 ÷ 8 = _____

4 72 ÷ 4 = _____   **9** 80 ÷ 8 = _____

5 80 ÷ 4 = _____   **10** 88 ÷ 8 = _____

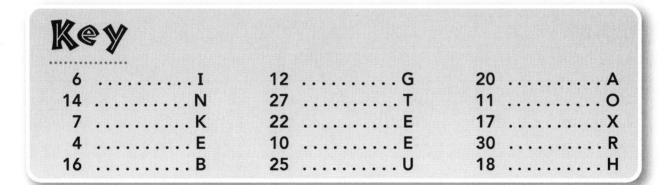

Key

6 I	12 . . . . G	20 . . . . A
14 . . . . N	27 . . . . T	11 . . . . O
7 . . . . K	22 . . . . E	17 X
4 . . . . E	10 . . . . E	30 . . . . R
16 . . . . B	25 . . . . U	18 . . . . H

Riddle Answer

T ___ ___   ___ ___ ___ - ___ ___ ___ ___ ___
  4 **8**   **3** **1** **9**   **7** **10** **2** **6** **5**

NAME _____   DATE _____

Riddle 16

Six cats sat in a boat. One jumped out. How many were left?

What To Do

Solve the division problems below. Match each quotient to a letter in the Key. Then write the letter in the space above its problem number to find the answer to the riddle.

1 72 ÷ 3 = _____   **6** 72 ÷ 9 = _____

2 78 ÷ 3 = _____   **7** 99 ÷ 9 = _____

3 99 ÷ 3 = _____   **8** 81 ÷ 9 = _____

4 87 ÷ 3 = _____   **9** 18 ÷ 9 = _____

5 54 ÷ 3 = _____   **10** 45 ÷ 9 = _____

Key

29 . . . . N	30 . . . . R	7 . . . . E
18 . . . . P	26 C	5 L
23 . . . . B	24 . . . . N	8 . . . . E
9 L	42 . . . . Z	22 . . . . F
11 . . . . Y	2 . . . . O	33 . . . . O

Riddle Answer

___ ___ ___ ___.   **They were a** ___ ___   ___ ___ ___ ___ **cats.**
1 **3** **4** **6**   **8** **10**   **2** **9** **5** **7**

NAME _____   DATE _____

Riddle 17

What has 12 legs, 6 eyes, 3 tails, and can't see?

What To Do

Solve the division problems below. Match each quotient to a letter in the Key. Then write the letter in the space above its problem number to find the answer to the riddle.

1 75 ÷ 5 = _____   **6** 84 ÷ 7 = _____

2 85 ÷ 5 = _____   **7** 98 ÷ 7 = _____

3 90 ÷ 5 = _____   **8** 77 ÷ 7 = _____

4 95 ÷ 5 = _____   **9** 91 ÷ 7 = _____

5 80 ÷ 5 = _____   **10** 56 ÷ 7 = _____

Key

8 L	15 .... B	17 .... N
20 .... Q	13 .... M	22 V
14 I	10 .... W	19 .... D
11 C	12 I	25 .... J
40 .... A	16 .... E	18 .... E

Riddle Answer

Thre ___   ___ ___ ___ ___ ___   ___ ___ ___ ___

5   **1** **10** **6** **2** **4**   **9** **7** **8** **3**

NAME _____   DATE _____

Riddle 18

What did the bee say to the flower?

What To Do

Solve the division problems below. Match each quotient to a letter in the Key. Then write the letter in the space above its problem number to find the answer to the riddle.

1 50 ÷ 1 = _____   **6** 60 ÷ 5 = _____

2 80 ÷ 4 = _____   **7** 40 ÷ 1 = _____

3 10 ÷ 2 = _____   **8** 20 ÷ 5 = _____

4 90 ÷ 3 = _____   **9** 30 ÷ 5 = _____

5 70 ÷ 7 = _____   **10** 90 ÷ 6 = _____

Key

11 . . . . K	5 . . . . N	20 . . . . S
50 . . . . Y	4 . . . . H	10 . . . . E
12 . . . . T	40 I	15 . . . . N
30 . . . . G	7 . . . . D	24 . . . . R
25 . . . . F	8 V	6 . . . . O

Riddle Answer

"Gree ___ ___ ___ ___ ___ , ___ ___ ___ ___ ___ !"

NAME _____ **DATE** _____

Riddle 19

What did the cat do when she wanted to buy something?

What To Do

Solve the division problems below. Match each quotient to a letter in the Key. Then write the letter in the space above its problem number to find the answer to the riddle.

1 $33 \div 3 =$ _____   **6** $32 \div 2 =$ _____

2 $96 \div 8 =$ _____   **7** $68 \div 4 =$ _____

3 $91 \div 7 =$ _____   **8** $18 \div 1 =$ _____

4 $84 \div 6 =$ _____   **9** $95 \div 5 =$ _____

5 $75 \div 5 =$ _____   **10** $80 \div 4 =$ _____

Key

21	K	13	A	24	P
14	S	16	O	15	U
18	G	11	L	12	C
20	E	28	Z	10	N
8	N	19	A	17	T

Riddle Answer

She read some __ __ __ - __ __ __ __ __ __ __ __.

NAME _____   DATE _____

Riddle 20

What did the hotel manager say to the elephant who couldn't pay her bill?

What To Do

Solve the division problems below. Match each quotient to a letter in the Key. Then write the letter in the space above its problem number to find the answer to the riddle.

1 2)33   **4** 3)10   **8** 9)14

2 4)70   **5** 7)20   **9** 6)23

3 5)23   **6** 6)17   **10** 4)31

7 8)45

Key

2 R6 . . . . N	17 R2 . . . . O	1 R4 . . . . Y
4 R1 . . . . M	7 R3 . . . . G	4 R3 . . . . T
3 R5 . . . . U	2 R4 L	5 R1 . . . . H
7 R4 . . . . B	5 R5 . . . . E	3 R1 . . . . T
16 R1 . . . . A	1 R5 . . . . D	2 R5 . . . . K

Riddle Answer

"Pack your trun ___ ___ ___ ___ ___ ___ ___ ___ ___ ___!"
    6   **1** **5** **8**   **10** **7** **4**   **2** **9** **3**

NAME_____   DATE_____

Riddle 21

Where do ants go when they are hungry?

What To Do

Solve the division problems below. Match each quotient to a letter in the Key. Then write the letter in the space above its problem number to find the answer to the riddle.

1 20)‾80‾   **4** 30)‾60‾   **8** 13)‾91‾

2 30)‾90‾   **5** 10)‾70‾   **9** 14)‾84‾

3 30)‾30‾   **6** 15)‾75‾   **10** 11)‾99‾

                       7 12)‾96‾

Key

8 .... R	14 .... K	1 .... S
10 .... W	9 .... T	26 .... Z
3 .... E	5 .... U	6 .... N
7 .... A	2 .... T	0 .... M
4 .... R	11 .... D	7 .... A

Riddle Answer

To a __ __ __ __ __ __ __ - __ __ __
  1 2 3 4 5 6 7   8 9 10

NAME_____ DATE_____

Riddle 22

What is as large as an elephant but weighs nothing?

What To Do

Solve the division problems below. Match each quotient to a letter in the Key. Then write the letter in the space above its problem number to find the answer to the riddle.

1 37)‾74‾   **4** 13)‾65‾   **8** 28)‾56‾

2 11)‾88‾   **5** 12)‾84‾   **9** 10)‾90‾

3 24)‾96‾   **6** 31)‾93‾   **10** 59)‾59‾

7 11)‾66‾

Key

7	W	12	G	0	R
2	A	8	N	6	O
10	E	11	F	13	V
1	S	9	S	3	H
5	T	2	A	4	D

Riddle Answer

An eleph __ __ __ __' __   __ __ __ __ __ __
  8 **2** **4** **10**   **9** **6** **1** **3** **7** **5**

NAME _____ DATE _____

Riddle 23

What happens when you cross a hen with a cement mixer?

What To Do

Solve the division problems below. Match each quotient to a letter in the Key. Then write the letter in the space above its problem number to find the answer to the riddle.

1 24)25   **4** 21)38   **8** 13)33

2 12)30   **5** 39)44   **9** 21)52

3 17)42   **6** 11)46   **10** 19)35

7 14)50

Key

1 R15 . . . . D	3 R8 . . . . . E	4 R3 . . . . . Q
1 R5 L	1 R1 . . . . . K	1 R16 . . . . B
2 R7 . . . . . R	3 R6 . . . . . N	2 R10 I
1 R4 . . . . . W	2 R6 . . . . . A	2 R8 C
4 R2 . . . . . R	1 R17 . . . . Y	6 R2 . . . . . S

Riddle Answer

You get a ___ ___ ___ ___ ___ ___ ___ ___ ___ ___.
    10 **6** **9** **3** **1**   **5** **2** **4** **7** **8**

NAME_____ DATE_____

Riddle 24

Why was Cinderella a poor baseball player?

What To Do

Solve the division problems below. Match each quotient to a letter in the Key. Then write the letter in the space above its problem number to find the answer to the riddle.

1 2)100   **4** 5)600   **8** 4)400

2 4)800   **5** 4)500   **9** 2)700

3 3)900   **6** 8)200   **10** 5)400

                      7 5)300

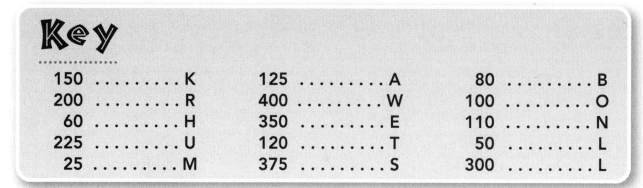

Key

150	. . . . K	125	. . . . A	80	. . . . B
200	. . . . R	400	. . . . W	100	. . . . O
60	. . . . H	350	. . . . E	110	. . . . N
225	. . . . U	120	. . . . T	50	 L
25	. . . . M	375	. . . . S	300	 L

Riddle Answer

She ran away f __ __ __   __ __ __   __ __ __ __.

2 8 6   4 7 9   10 5 3 1

NAME _____   DATE _____

Riddle 25

Why did the elephant eat the candle?

What To Do

Solve the division problems below. Match each quotient to a letter in the Key. Then write the letter in the space above its problem number to find the answer to the riddle.

1 $2\overline{)120}$ **4** $4\overline{)100}$ **8** $8\overline{)288}$

2 $2\overline{)148}$ **5** $4\overline{)256}$ **9** $8\overline{)264}$

3 $2\overline{)192}$ **6** $4\overline{)204}$ **10** $8\overline{)176}$

7 $4\overline{)184}$

Key

36 ....T	18 ....F	22 ....H
25 I	64 ....T	74 ....T
33 ....G	51 ....O	44 ....W
29 ....U	46 ....A	21 ....N
60 L	41 ....K	96 ....E

Riddle Answer

She wanted something __ __ __ __ __   __ __   __ __ __ .

1 **4** **9** **10** **5**   **8** **6**   **3** **7** **2**

NAME_____ DATE _____

Riddle 26

What did the doctor give the elephant who couldn't sleep?

What To Do

Solve the division problems below. Match each quotient to a letter in the Key. Then write the letter in the space above its problem number to find the answer to the riddle.

1 3)‾204‾   **4** 6)‾126‾   **8** 9)‾405‾

2 3)‾126‾   **5** 6)‾210‾   **9** 9)‾270‾

3 3)‾294‾   **6** 6)‾240‾   **10** 9)‾306‾

7 6)‾264‾

Key

46	. . . . A	30	. . . . U	39	 C
44	. . . . Z	68	. . . . U	35	. . . . K
21	. . . . N	53	. . . . P	40	 I
98	. . . . R	34	. . . . E	38	. . . . D
25	. . . . M	42	 L	45	 I

Riddle Answer:

A tr __ __ __ - q __ __ __ __ __ __ __ __
   1 **4** **5**   **9** **8** **2** **6** **7** **10** **3**

NAME _____ DATE _____

Riddle 27

Where do bees wait for public transportation?

What To Do

Solve the division problems below. Match each quotient to a letter in the Key. Then write the letter in the space above its problem number to find the answer to the riddle.

1 1)166   **4** 5)350   **8** 7)280

2 5)150   **5** 5)110   **9** 7)294

3 5)220   **6** 1)245   **10** 5)250

7 7)364

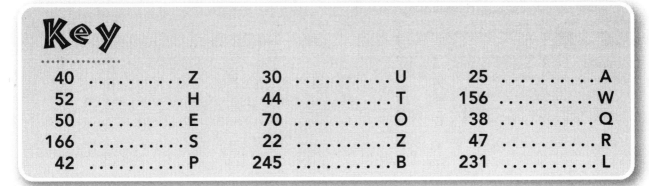

Key

40 ....Z	30 ....U	25 ....A
52 ....H	44 ....T	156 ....W
50 ....E	70 ....O	38 ....Q
166 ....S	22 ....Z	47 ....R
42 ....P	245 ....B	231 L

Riddle Answer

At t ___ ___   " ___ ___ ___ ___ "   ___ ___ ___ ___

  7 **10**   **6** **2** **5** **8**   **1** **3** **4** **9**

NAME_____ DATE_____

Riddle 28

What's the difference between a fish and a piano?

What To Do

Solve the division problems below. Match each quotient to a letter in the Key. Then write the letter in the space above its problem number to find the answer to the riddle.

1 4)360   **4** 5)115   **8** 5)385

2 7)112   **5** 6)108   **9** 3)105

3 9)216   **6** 2)130   **10** 7)133

7 6)120

Key

23 . . . . S	90 . . . . T	31 . . . . P
60 . . . . E	39 . . . . M	19 . . . . U
35 . . . . F	65 . . . . N	16 I
24 . . . . A	40 . . . . A	77 . . . . T
55 . . . . R	20 . . . . H	18 . . . . N

Riddle Answer

You ca ___'___ " ___ ___ ___ ___ ___" ___ ___ ___ ___.
     5 **8**   **1** **10** **6** **3**   **9** **2** **4** **7**

DATE _____

e ant
d at
p to be?

What To Do

...w. Match each quotient to a letter in the Key. Then write ...the space above its problem number to find the answer to the riddle.

①   5)226   **④**   4)126   **⑧**   8)162

②   8)108   **⑤**   6)320   **⑨**   5)252

③   7)404   **⑥**   3)148   **⑩**   9)380

           ⑦   7)136

Key

45 R1	T	42 R2	U	49 R1	C
17 R3	M	10 R8	V	30 R7	K
53 R2	C	19 R3	T	31 R2	N
57 R5	A	22 R1	L	19 R2	B
50 R2	A	13 R4	N	20 R2	O

Riddle Answer

An ___ ___ ___ ___ ___ ___ ___ - ___ ___ ___
   ⑨   ⑥   ⑤   ⑧   ⑩   ②   ①   ③   ④   ⑦

NAME _____ DATE _____

Riddle 30

Why did the computer act loony?

What To Do

Solve the division problems below. Match each quotient to a letter in the Key. Then write the letter in the space above its problem number to find the answer to the riddle.

1 10)110   **4** 10)180   **8** 10)170

2 10)140   **5** 10)160   **9** 10)120

3 10)200   **6** 10)190   **10** 10)150

7 10)130

Key

11 . . . . O	16 . . . . W	19 . . . . S
14 . . . . E	24 . . . . P	35 . . . . D
22 . . . . A	13 L	29 . . . . F
12 . . . . O	17 . . . . E	20 . . . . S
15 C	30 . . . . N	18 . . . . R

Riddle Answer

It had s __ __ __ __ __   __ __ __ __ __.

NAME _____   DATE _____

Riddle 31

What is the largest ant in the jungle?

What To Do

Solve the division problems below. Match each quotient to a letter in the Key. Then write the letter in the space above its problem number to find the answer to the riddle.

1 $45\overline{)135}$ **4** $40\overline{)200}$ **8** $10\overline{)900}$

2 $25\overline{)100}$ **5** $50\overline{)300}$ **9** $20\overline{)220}$

3 $30\overline{)300}$ **6** $60\overline{)420}$ **10** $30\overline{)360}$

7 $30\overline{)240}$

Key

6 . . . . A	1 . . . . D	10 . . . . P
12 . . . . H	60 . . . . B	5 . . . . E
21 C	11 . . . . N	50 . . . . S
3 . . . . N	13 . . . . O	7 . . . . E
90 . . . . T	4 . . . . A	8 L

Riddle Answer

___ ___ ___ ___ ___ ___ ___ - ___ ___ ___
5 **9** **4** **7** **6** **3** **10** **2** **1** **8**

NAME _____ DATE _____

Riddle 32

What did the other elephants call the flying elephant?

What To Do

Solve the division problems below. Match each quotient to a letter in the Key. Then write the letter in the space above its problem number to find the answer to the riddle.

1 12)180   **4** 16)208   **8** 32)192

2 22)198   **5** 24)288   **9** 44)176

3 14)196   **6** 36)180   **10** 52)156

7 18)198

Key

12 . . . . U		1 C		14 . . . . H	
24 . . . . W		5 . . . . E		17 . . . . K	
15 . . . . T		7 . . . . A		9 . . . . J	
11 . . . . O		6 . . . . E		3 . . . . J	
4 . . . . M		10 I		13 . . . . B	

Riddle Answer

T __ __   __ __ __ __ __   __ __ __
3 **6**   **2** **5** **9** **4** **7**   **10** **8** **1**

NAME _____ DATE _____

Riddle 33

What did the adult bee say to the kid bee who was in trouble?

What To Do

Solve the division problems below. Match each quotient to a letter in the Key. Then write the letter in the space above its problem number to find the answer to the riddle.

❶ 13)195   ❹ 19)228   ❽ 29)174

❷ 15)165   ❺ 25)225   ❾ 31)248

❸ 27)189   ❻ 39)156   ❿ 37)185

❼ 43)129

Key

10	B	2	D	15	V
9	E	5	U	20	K
14	C	11	H	4	Y
7	E	6	I	12	E
8	R	18	G	3	O

Riddle Answer

"B ___ ___ – ___ ___ ___ ___   ___ ___ ___ ___ self!"

❸ ❺   ❷ ❽ ❶ ❹   ❻ ❼ ❿ ❾

NAME _____ DATE _____

Riddle 34

What can a circle do that a half circle can never do?

What To Do

Solve the division problems below. Match each quotient to a letter in the Key. Then write the letter in the space above its problem number to find the answer to the riddle.

1 4)2,000   **4** 5)1,500   **8** 3)2,400

2 5)3,000   **5** 2)5,000   **9** 2)1,400

3 2)4,000   **6** 4)6,000   **10** 5)9,000

7 3)1,200

Key

600 . . . . R	2,500 . . . . D	500 . . . . O
800 . . . . U	400 . . . . N	900 . . . . S
1,000 . . . . A	100 . . . . M	3,000 . . . . Y
200 . . . . G	1,500 . . . . O	700 . . . . O
300 L	2,000 . . . . K	250 . . . . E

Riddle Answer

___ ___ ___ ___   ___ ___ ___ ___ ___
4 **9** **1** **3**   **2** **6** **8** **7** **5**

NAME _____   DATE _____

Riddle 35

What game do fish like to play?

What To Do

Solve the division problems below. Match each quotient to a letter in the Key. Then write the letter in the space above its problem number to find the answer to the riddle.

1 10)‾2,000‾   **4** 20)‾1,200‾   **8** 30)‾9,000‾

2 20)‾8,000‾   **5** 10)‾7,000‾   **9** 20)‾1,600‾

3 30)‾1,500‾   **6** 10)‾1,000‾   **10** 30)‾2,100‾

7 20)‾1,800‾

Key

100	. . . . T	200	. . . . M	800	. . . . R
300	. . . . T	150	. . . . J	60	. . . . N
50	. . . . A	70	. . . . H	90	. . . . U
110	. . . . O	700	. . . . E	20	. . . . W
80	. . . . T	120	. . . . K	400	. . . . A

Riddle Answer

Na __ __   __ __ __ __   __ __ __ __

NAME _____ DATE _____

Riddle 36

What do you call a sleeping bull?

What To Do

Answer the questions below. Match each answer to a letter in the Key. Then write the letter in the space above its problem number to find the answer to the riddle.

1 How many hours are there in 60 minutes? _____

2 How many hours are there in 180 minutes? _____

3 How many hours are there in 240 minutes? _____

4 How many hours are there in 360 minutes? _____

5 How many hours are there in 120 minutes? _____

6 How many hours are there in 300 minutes? _____

7 How many hours are there in 720 minutes? _____

8 How many hours are there in 600 minutes? _____

9 How many hours are there in 900 minutes? _____

10 How many minutes are there in half an hour? _____

Key

2 hours . . . . . Z	7 hours L	6 hours L
4 hours . . . . A	10 hours . . . . . D	15 hours . . . . U
8 hours . . . . . O	3 hours . . . . . R	20 minutes . . . . . D
30 minutes L	20 hours . . . . . B	45 minutes . . . . . E
1 hour . . . . . O	12 hours . . . . . E	5 hours . . . . . B

Riddle Answer

__ __ __ __ __ - __ __ __ __ __ __
3   **6** **9** **4** **10**   **8** **1** **5** **7** **2**

NAME _____   DATE _____

Riddle 37

Why was the veterinarian overworked?

What To Do

Answer the questions below. Match each answer to a letter in the Key. Then write the letter in the space above its problem number to find the answer to the riddle.

1 How many weeks are there in 14 days? _____

2 How many weeks are there in 28 days? _____

3 How many weeks are there in 35 days? _____

4 How many weeks are there in 56 days? _____

5 How many weeks are there in 77 days? _____

6 How many weeks are there in 49 days? _____

7 How many weeks are there in 98 days? _____

8 How many weeks are there in 140 days? _____

9 How many weeks are there in 175 days? _____

10 How many weeks are there in 133 days? _____

Key

1 week I	6 weeks . . . . . J	19 weeks . . . . . S
7 weeks . . . . . G	11 weeks . . . . . A	8 weeks . . . . . D
20 weeks . . . . . A	2 weeks . . . . . T	4 weeks . . . . . D
5 weeks . . . . . S	25 weeks . . . . . O	10 weeks . . . . . K
15 weeks . . . . . E	3 weeks V	14 weeks . . . . . N

Riddle Answer

It was raining c ___ ___ ___   ___ ___ ___ ___   ___ ___ ___ ___.
      8   **1** **10**   **5** **7** **2**   **4** **9** **6** **3**

NAME_____ DATE _____

Riddle 38

What game do mice like to play?

What To Do

Solve the problems below. Match each answer to a letter in the Key.
Then write the letter in the space above its problem to find the answer to the riddle.

1 Two pieces of gum cost 50 cents. How much does one piece of gum cost? _____

2 Three bags of popcorn cost $3.00. How much does one bag of popcorn cost? _____

3 Four coloring books cost $8.00. How much does one coloring book cost? _____

4 Five pencils cost $1.50. How much does one pencil cost? _____

5 Six notebooks cost $15.00. How much does one notebook cost? _____

6 Seven ice-cream cones cost $21.00. How much does one ice-cream cone cost? _____

7 Eight T-shirts cost $80.00. How much does one T-shirt cost? _____

8 Nine movie tickets cost $72.00. How much does one movie ticket cost? _____

9 Ten magazines cost $40.00. How much does one magazine cost? _____

10 Fifteen erasers cost $5.25. How much does one eraser cost? _____

Key

$10.00 . . . . . . K	$3.00 . . . . . . H	35 cents . . . . . . S
$8.00 I	$1.50 . . . . . . A	$3.50 . . . . . . Z
50 cents . . . . . . N	$5.00 C	$2.50 . . . . . . Q
$1.00 . . . . . . D	$2.00 . . . . . . A	$4.00 . . . . . . E
30 cents . . . . . . E	25 cents . . . . . . U	75 cents I

Riddle Answer

___ ___ ___ ___ **and** ___ ___ ___ ___ ___ ___
6 **8** **2** **9**   **10** **5** **1** **4** **3** **7**

NAME _____ DATE _____

Riddle 39

Why is it hard to play a joke on a snake?

What To Do

Solve the problems below. Match each answer to a letter in the Key.
Then write the letter in the space above its problem to find the answer to the riddle.

1 Debbie has 4 apples. John has half as many apples as Debbie has. How many apples does John have? _____

2 Donovan has 9 oranges. Dana has one-third as many oranges as Donovan has. How many oranges does Dana have? _____

3 Chris has 20 grapes. Tony has one-fifth as many grapes as Chris has. How many grapes does Tony have? _____

4 Patty has 30 markers. Mark has one-sixth as many markers as Patty has. How many markers does Mark have? _____

5 Lilly has 24 stickers. Olivia has one-fourth as many stickers as Lilly has. How many stickers does Olivia have? _____

6 Leah has 10 comic books. Bob has one-tenth as many comic books as Leah has. How many comic books does Bob have? _____

7 Max has 42 magnets. Hannah has one-third as many magnets as Max has. How many magnets does Hannah have? _____

8 Emma has 32 blocks. Kara has half has many blocks as Emma has. How many blocks does Kara have? _____

9 Maureen has 60 marbles. Michael has one-sixth as many marbles as Maureen has. How many marbles does Michael have? _____

10 Peter has 81 sticks. Ilan has one-ninth as many sticks as Peter has. How many sticks does Ilan have? _____

Key

20	K
14	G
6	L
7	A
5	U
2	L
16	P
8	M
1	I
18	O
4	T
9	S
12	R
10	E
3	L

Riddle Answer

You can't ___ ___ ___ ___ ___ ___ ___ ___ ___ ___.

NAME _____ DATE _____

Riddle 40   Why couldn't the piano player open the piano?

What To Do

Solve the problems below. Match each answer to a letter in the Key.
Then write the letter in the space above its problem to find the answer to the riddle.

1 Chen scored 10 points in 2 basketball games. He scored the same number of points in each game. How many points did he score in each game? _____

2 Maria scored 6 goals in 6 soccer games. She scored the same number of goals in each game. How many goals did she score in each game? _____

3 Isaiah scored 30 points in 10 basketball games. He scored the same number of points in each game. How many points did he score in each game? _____

4 Yoshi scored 28 goals in 14 soccer games. He scored the same number of goals in each game. How many goals did he score in each game? _____

5 Mitzi scored 300 points in 30 basketball games. She scored the same number of points in each game. How many points did she score in each game? _____

6 Ron scored 210 goals in 35 soccer games. What was the average number of goals he scored over those games? _____

7 Alonzo scored 75 points in 5 basketball games. What was the average number of points he scored over those games? _____

8 Louise scored 27 goals in 9 soccer games. What was the average number of goals she scored over those games? _____

9 Russell scored 176 points in 22 basketball games. What was the average number of points he scored over those games? _____

10 Kadisha scored 205 goals in 41 soccer games. What was the average number of goals she scored over those games? _____

Key

6 points . . .	A
15 goals . . .	T
2 goals . . .	E
10 points . .	N
1 point . . .	W
3 goals . . .	Y
15 points . .	D
5 points . . .	S
6 goals	S
2 points . . .	C
5 goals	I
8 points . . .	I
1 goal	K
3 points . . .	E
10 goals . .	O

Riddle Answer   The ___ ___ ___ ___ were ___ ___ ___ ___ ___ ___.
2 **3** **8** **6**   **10** **5** **1** **9** **7** **4**

Answers

Riddle 1 (page 5)
1. 1
2. 4
3. 3
4. 9
5. 7
6. 2
7. 8
8. 6
9. 5
10. 10

Why is heat faster than cold?
You can catch a cold.

Riddle 2 (page 6)
1. 3
2. 1
3. 5
4. 2
5. 7
6. 9
7. 4
8. 6
9. 8
10. 10

Why do bats always stay in groups?
They like to hang together.

Riddle 3 (page 7)
1. 1
2. 2
3. 3
4. 4
5. 5
6. 6
7. 7
8. 8
9. 9
10. 10

Why did the golfer carry extra socks?
In case she got a hole in one

Riddle 4 (page 8)
1. 2
2. 1
3. 6
4. 9
5. 3
6. 8
7. 10
8. 4
9. 7
10. 5

Why did the witch's hair stay in place?
She put on scare spray.

Riddle 5 (page 9)
1. 7
2. 2
3. 6
4. 5
5. 4
6. 1
7. 9
8. 3
9. 8
10. 10

Why is a fish easy to weigh?
It has its own scales.

Riddle 6 (page 10)
1. 2
2. 1
3. 10
4. 8
5. 3
6. 9
7. 6
8. 4
9. 5
10. 7

What did the bees put on when they were cold?
Their yellow jackets

Riddle 7 (page 11)
1. 5
2. 7
3. 4
4. 9
5. 8
6. 2
7. 10
8. 1
9. 3
10. 6

Why did the pig break into the house?
He was a ham-burglar.

Riddle 8 (page 12)
1. 9
2. 7
3. 4
4. 1
5. 2
6. 8
7. 3
8. 6
9. 10
10. 5

How do elephants talk to one another?
They use 'elephones.

Riddle 9 (page 13)
1. 4
2. 1
3. 5
4. 10
5. 7
6. 2
7. 3
8. 9
9. 6
10. 8

How did people greet the boy who was named after his father?
Howdy, Daddy!

Riddle 10 (page 14)
1. 5
2. 7
3. 10
4. 9
5. 4
6. 8
7. 2
8. 3
9. 1
10. 6

Why did the Girl Scout get dizzy?
**She spent all day
doing good turns.**

Riddle 11 (page 15)
1. 22
2. 27
3. 31
4. 29
5. 33
6. 36
7. 38
8. 26
9. 32
10. 39

Why did the chicken cross
the Internet?
**It wanted to get to the other
site.**

Riddle 12 (page 16)
1. 12
2. 15
3. 17
4. 18
5. 20
6. 11
7. 14
8. 13
9. 16
10. 19

Why did the bee hum?
It forgot the song's words.

Riddle 13 (page 17)
1. 25
2. 36
3. 21
4. 28
5. 27
6. 11
7. 13
8. 15

9. 12
10. 14

Why did the bird visit the library?
It was looking for bookworms.

Riddle 14 (page 18)
1. 12
2. 30
3. 18
4. 20
5. 14
6. 11
7. 13
8. 15
9. 17
10. 19

Why was the girl worried
when her nose grew to be
11 inches long?
**She thought it might
turn into a foot.**

Riddle 15 (page 19)
1. 22
2. 14
3. 16
4. 18
5. 20
6. 6
7. 12
8. 4
9. 10
10. 11

Which flower did the bee
like best?
The bee-gonia

Riddle 16 (page 20)
1. 24
2. 26
3. 33
4. 29
5. 18
6. 8
7. 11
8. 9
9. 2
10. 5

Six cats sat in a boat.
One jumped out. How many
were left?
None. They were all copycats.

Riddle 17 (page 21)
1. 15
2. 17
3. 18
4. 19
5. 16
6. 12
7. 14
8. 11
9. 13
10. 8

What has 12 legs, 6 eyes, 3 tails,
and can't see?
Three blind mice

Riddle 18 (page 22)
1. 50
2. 20
3. 5
4. 30
5. 10
6. 12
7. 40
8. 4
9. 6
10. 15

What did the bee say to the
flower?
"Greetings, honey!"

Riddle 19 (page 23)
1. 11
2. 12
3. 13
4. 14
5. 15
6. 16
7. 17
8. 18
9. 19
10. 20

What did the cat do when she
wanted to buy something?
She read some cat-alogues.

Riddle 20 (page 24)
1. 16 R1
2. 17 R2
3. 4 R3
4. 3 R1
5. 2 R6
6. 2 R5
7. 5 R5
8. 1 R5

9. 3 R5
10. 7 R3

What did the hotel manager say to the elephant who couldn't pay her bill?
"Pack your trunk and get out!"

Riddle 21 (page 25)
  1. 4
  2. 3
  3. 1
  4. 2
  5. 7
  6. 5
  7. 8
  8. 7
  9. 6
  10. 9

Where do ants go when they are hungry?
To a restaur-ant

Riddle 22 (page 26)
  1. 2
  2. 8
  3. 4
  4. 5
  5. 7
  6. 3
  7. 6
  8. 2
  9. 9
  10. 1

What is as large as an elephant but weighs nothing?
An elephant's shadow

Riddle 23 (page 27)
  1. 1 R1
  2. 2 R6
  3. 2 R8
  4. 1 R17
  5. 1 R5
  6. 4 R2
  7. 3 R8
  8. 2 R7
  9. 2 R10
  10. 1 R16

What happens when you cross a hen with a cement mixer?
You get a brick layer.

Riddle 24 (page 28)
  1. 50
  2. 200
  3. 300
  4. 120
  5. 125
  6. 25
  7. 60
  8. 100
  9. 350
  10. 80

Why was Cinderella a poor baseball player?
She ran away from the ball.

Riddle 25 (page 29)
  1. 60
  2. 74
  3. 96
  4. 25
  5. 64
  6. 51
  7. 46
  8. 36
  9. 33
  10. 22

Why did the elephant eat the candle?
She wanted something light to eat.

Riddle 26 (page 30)
  1. 68
  2. 42
  3. 98
  4. 21
  5. 35
  6. 40
  7. 44
  8. 45
  9. 30
  10. 34

What did the doctor give the elephant who couldn't sleep?
A trunk-quilizer

Riddle 27 (page 31)
  1. 166
  2. 30
  3. 44
  4. 70
  5. 22
  6. 245
  7. 52

8. 40
9. 42
10. 50

Where do bees wait for public transportation?
At the "buzz" stop

Riddle 28 (Page 32)
  1. 90
  2. 16
  3. 24
  4. 23
  5. 18
  6. 65
  7. 20
  8. 77
  9. 35
  10. 19

What's the difference between a fish and a piano?
You can't "tuna" fish.

Riddle 29 (page 33)
  1. 45 R1
  2. 13 R4
  3. 57 R5
  4. 31 R2
  5. 53 R2
  6. 49 R1
  7. 19 R3
  8. 20 R2
  9. 50 R2
  10. 42 R2

What did the ant who was good at math grow up to be?
An account-ant

Riddle 30 (page 34)
  1. 11
  2. 14
  3. 20
  4. 18
  5. 16
  6. 19
  7. 13
  8. 17
  9. 12
  10. 15

Why did the computer act loony?
It had screws loose.

Riddle 31 (page 35)
1. 3
2. 4
3. 10
4. 5
5. 6
6. 7
7. 8
8. 90
9. 11
10. 12

What is the largest ant in the jungle?
An eleph-ant

Riddle 32 (page 36)
1. 15
2. 9
3. 14
4. 13
5. 12
6. 5
7. 11
8. 6
9. 4
10. 3

What did the other elephants call the flying elephant?
The jumbo jet

Riddle 33 (page 37)
1. 15
2. 11
3. 7
4. 12
5. 9
6. 4
7. 3
8. 6
9. 8
10. 5

What did the adult bee say to the kid bee who was in trouble?
"Bee–hive yourself!"

Riddle 34 (page 38)
1. 500
2. 600
3. 2,000
4. 300
5. 2,500
6. 1,500
7. 400
8. 800
9. 700
10. 1,800

What can a circle do that a half circle can never do?
Look round

Riddle 35 (page 39)
1. 200
2. 400
3. 50
4. 60
5. 700
6. 100
7. 90
8. 300
9. 80
10. 70

What game do fish like to play?
Name that tuna

Riddle 36 (page 40)
1. 1 hour
2. 3 hours
3. 4 hours
4. 6 hours
5. 2 hours
6. 5 hours
7. 12 hours
8. 10 hours
9. 15 hours
10. 30 minutes

What do you call a sleeping bull?
A bull-dozer

Riddle 37 (page 41)
1. 2 weeks
2. 4 weeks
3. 5 weeks
4. 8 weeks
5. 11 weeks
6. 7 weeks
7. 14 weeks
8. 20 weeks

9. 25 weeks
10. 19 weeks

Why was the veterinarian overworked?
It was raining cats and dogs.

Riddle 38 (page 42)
1. 25 cents
2. $1.00
3. $2.00
4. 30 cents
5. $2.50
6. $3.00
7. $10.00
8. $8.00
9. $4.00
10. 35 cents

What game do mice like to play?
Hide and squeak

Riddle 39 (page 43)
1. 2 apples
2. 3 oranges
3. 4 grapes
4. 5 markers
5. 6 stickers
6. 1 comic book
7. 14 magnets
8. 16 blocks
9. 10 marbles
10. 9 sticks

Why is it hard to play a joke on a snake?
You can't pull its leg.

Riddle 40 (page 44)
1. 5 points
2. 1 goal
3. 3 points
4. 2 goals
5. 10 points
6. 6 goals
7. 15 points
8. 3 goals
9. 8 points
10. 5 goals

Why couldn't the piano player open the piano?
The keys were inside.